GHOST
writer

by David Tristram

Ed
A_____
Ruby
Glenda
Frances
Hedley

GW00746075

You'll find more information on Flying Ducks Publications on our webbed site:

www.DavidTristram.Playwright.com
e-mail: DavidTristram@Playwright.com

ISBN 1 900997 02 9

Flying Ducks Publications, Station Road, Highley, Shropshire, WV16 6NW

ACT ONE

The setting is Edward's scruffy bedsit, which is an upstairs attic room within Alex's flat. The stage is black. A shadowy figure is sat on a packing case at a small writing table. An anglepoise lamp is switched on, eerily up-lighting the face of Edward, who stares into space with a look of grim foreboding. He begins to utter some famous words:

Edward To be, or not to be, that is the question.
 Whether it is nobler in the mind to suffer
 the slings and arrows of outrageous fortune,
 Or to take arms against a sea of troubles,
 And by opposing end them? To die, to sleep,
 No more; and by a sleep to say we end
 The heartache and the thousand natural shocks
 That flesh is heir to,-'tis a consummation
 Devoutly to be wish'd. To die, to sleep.

He addresses the last few words to a black revolver, which he has lifted ominously into the light. He stares nervously down its barrel, hands shaking, before placing it into his mouth and closing his eyes. At that critical moment, with the tension unbearable, the lights come crashing on, to reveal Alex at the doorway.

Alex Boo!
Edward (*shocked, pulling the gun down to his side*) Jesus, Alex! You certainly pick
 your moments.
Alex What were you doing in the dark? Or shouldn't I ask? You'll ruin your eyes,
 you know. I'm out of booze - do you mind?

A Flying Ducks Publication

Edward Help yourself.

Alex opens a wardrobe. From top to bottom, it is crammed full of gin bottles. He plucks one out and starts unscrewing the cap.

Alex Do you want one?
Edward Yes, I think I probably do.

Alex takes a second bottle from the wardrobe and tosses it to Edward, before taking a huge swig from his own bottle.

Alex Mind if I join you?
Edward Pull up a packing case.
Alex You all right?
Edward Fine.
Alex You look a bit pale. Perhaps you should see a doctor.
Edward I think I was about to.

They sit in silence for a moment, both swigging from their bottles.

Alex Listen, I was er...hoping you and I could have a bit of a chat.
Edward Chat away.
Alex Look, don't take this the wrong way.
Edward You're kicking me out.
Alex I am not kicking you out! How could you say that?
Edward I can't go back to that house, Alex.
Alex No-one's asking you to go back to that house. I'm not asking you to go anywhere. I like having you here. You're a...fun guy. Whose idea was it for you to stay here in the first place, eh?
Edward Mine.
Alex Okay, but whose idea was it for me to agree?
Edward Mine.
Alex All right. But I'm used to it now. Look, I'm your friend, right? I'm just concerned about you. You look a bit, well, down.
Edward Don't worry. I'll sort myself out.
Alex Moping around a bedsit all night. It's not good for you. When was the last time you went out - to the pub, or the pictures, or a restaurant?
Edward Last night. I went to the Chinese takeaway.
Alex You need a girlfriend.

Edward Hah! Look who's talking.

Alex Hey, now come on. Don't start gay-bashing. You know what I mean.

Edward I've had girlfriends.

Alex You've had women. You need a girlfriend.

Edward I'm too busy.

Alex Doing what? (*Momentarily enthused*) Have you started writing again?

Edward No.

Alex You need to write. A writer needs to write. Why don't you knock off a quick comedy thriller or something - just to get the old juices going again?

Edward Act One. The dead body of a writer lies next to a smoking revolver.

Alex Yes, that's the sort of thing.

Edward I'll see what I can do.

Alex Good man. (*Taking a big swig from his gin bottle*) And that's another thing. You drink too much. What are you doing with my gun?

Edward I was going to shoot myself with it.

Alex (*casually*) Oh, really?

Edward I had it in my mouth. I was about to pull the trigger when you came bursting in.

Alex You don't want to do that. That would hurt.

Edward I thought it might stop the hurt.

Alex (*suddenly sensing that Edward is not joking*) My God, you're serious.

Edward Deadly.

Alex Come here! (*Alex clutches Edward in a manly, emotional hug. Both men are fighting back tears*) You stupid, stupid, sod.

Edward I know.

Alex Why didn't you come and talk to me?

Edward It's one year ago today, Alex.

Alex I know. I know.

Edward God, I miss her!

Alex Look, Ruby is gone! She's never coming back. And you're not following her. What happened happened, okay? It wasn't pleasant, but it's finished. Dead and buried.

Edward It was my fault.

Alex (*angrily shaking the almost hysterical Edward*) It was not your fault! Stop talking like that! It was not your fault. It was nobody's fault except her own, do you hear? And I'm not going to sit by and watch you destroy the rest of your life grieving over a woman like that.

Edward What do you mean - a woman like that?

Alex Oh, come on! Is your memory so bad? You two weren't exactly Mr and Mrs

Happy, remember?

Edward It was just a bit stormy.

Alex Stormy? It was a bloody hurricane. The only reason your marriage lasted so long was that you couldn't agree on the terms of the divorce.

Edward We just had very strong feelings about each other.

Alex That was hatred! You hated each other. She hated you. You detested her.

Edward No!

Alex Yes!

Edward That's...that's too strong a word.

Alex Oh, really? (*He produces a piece of paper from his wallet*)

Edward What's that?

Alex This never leaves my wallet. Do you recognize it? This is the letter you asked me to keep quiet about at the coroner's inquest.

Edward All right, all right.

Alex (*reading from the letter*) "I hate her. I hate the bitch. I couldn't hate her more if she stuck pins in my eyes. All I want to do is strangle her, and drop her body in a vat of acid, but that would be too good for her. I hate her. I hate her. I hate her. I hate her."

Edward You've made your point.

Alex It goes on to say how much you hated her.

Edward She still haunts me, Alex.

Alex Look, whatever it is you're bottling up in there, it's got to come out. Would it help to talk?

Edward You don't like me talking about her.

Alex If it helps exorcise the ghost, let's talk about her.

Edward We were amazing together.

Alex Amazing. Yeah, that's one word.

Edward We had this amazing...sexual chemistry.

Alex This is the woman who superglued glitter to your bollocks.

Edward She was just mad at me. She thought I'd been sleeping around.

Alex And had you?

Edward Up until that point, yes. Okay, so she was a bit overdramatic - you know what actresses are like.

Alex I know she hated you.

Edward You're not going to let that drop, are you?

Alex It's a fact. And her dying doesn't change that. She's gone, Edward. And you need a girlfriend. One who's alive. One you won't hate. One you might even like.

Edward How can I think about other women?

Alex Don't worry. Leave that to me.

Edward What's that supposed to mean?

Alex That little chat I wanted. Promise you won't shout at me.

Edward I'm going to shout at you.

Alex Look, I think you need some female company.

Edward Tell me you haven't.

Alex I have.

Edward Oh, Alex, no!

Alex An actress friend of mine.

Edward No!

Alex Glenda.

Edward No!

Alex She's just got divorced.

Edward No!

Alex Now before you say anything, she's...

Edward No!

Alex Look, before you say no....

Edward No!

Alex She's a great girl, Edward...

Edward No!

Alex A good-looking girl...

Edward No!

Alex Bags of fun.

Edward No!

Alex You'll have a great time together.

Edward (*picking up the gun*) I'm going to have to shoot you, Alex.

Alex Hey, come on - look at me! I'm your best friend. Now would I set you up with a dragon?

Edward You're hardly an expert in the opposite sex, are you, Alex?

Alex Just because I don't play the game, it doesn't mean I don't know the rules. She's a cracker, Edward. Trust me. And she's straight.

Edward Oh, a real bonus.

Alex Look, if you're going to get bitchy...

Edward I can't believe you've done this without asking me.

Alex And if I'd have asked you, what would you have said?

Edward You don't understand, Alex.

Alex I do understand.

Edward I need time to myself.

Alex (*taking the gun*) This is what happens when you get time to yourself. You've had a year. Now let it go! (*Edward slumps onto the bed*) Look, see Glenda. Just for one night. If you don't hit it off, I'll never say another word about it.

Edward No.

Alex So, you'll think it over. (*No response*) Edward, look at me. I've just saved your life.

Edward I know.

Alex Okay. This is how you pay me back.

Edward When?

Alex Tomorrow night. Eight o'clock.

Edward Where?

Alex Here.

Edward Here? Why here?

Alex Because I wanted to make sure you'd show up. Don't worry, I've already warned her that it's a complete shitheap. She doesn't mind.

Edward Thanks.

Alex (*looking at the gun*) I can't believe you were really going to do this.

Edward Neither can I. But I think I was, Alex. I really think I was. Go on, say it.

Alex What?

Edward The old cliché. This wouldn't solve anything.

Alex It wouldn't. It's not a real gun.

Edward Isn't it?

Alex It's a stage prop. What would I be doing with a real gun?

Edward Dunno. I wasn't thinking clearly.

Alex All this would do is singe your tongue and stain your underpants. Two problems you could do without. Say "Yes" to Glenda. Please. For me.

Edward Yes to Glenda.

Alex Good man.

Edward One condition.

Alex Name it.

Edward No more matchmaking.

Alex I gave you my word.

Edward Remember what happened the last time you introduced me to someone.

Alex I know, you married her. But Glenda's different. You'll like her. Trust me, I'm a doctor.

Edward No, you're not.

Alex All right, I'm an actor pretending to be a doctor.

Edward Goodnight, Alex.

Alex Thanks for the drink. Oh, nearly forgot, can I borrow some money?

Edward What, again?

A Flying Ducks Publication

Alex I need it to pay off a debt.
Edward How much this time?
Alex Fifty?
Edward Bedside cabinet.
Alex You're a star. (*He grabs the gin bottle, drops the gun on the bedside cabinet, and rifles through the drawer*) There's only thirty quid.
Edward Sorry, I'll have to owe you the rest.
Alex Don't worry, I still owe you twenty from last time. We'll call it quits.
Edward Thanks.
Alex (*spotting a packet of pills in the bedside drawer*) What are these?
Edward Sleeping pills. It's all right, I'm not going to do anything stupid. I need to sleep, Alex.

He examines the blister packs, stuffs one mainly-used one back into the outer packet, and slips the rest into his pocket.

Alex I'll leave you one.

Alex makes for the door.

Edward Alex.....thanks.

Alex nods, and exits. Edward sighs. He moves to his typewriter, inserts a piece of paper, and sits staring at it for a few moments. Angrily devoid of inspiration, he finally tears out the paper, screws it up and tosses it away. Clearly depressed and tired, he takes an enormous swig from his bottle, switches on a bedside lamp, switches off the main room light, and sinks onto the bed, staring into space.

Edward Now cracks a noble heart. (*Restless, he looks over at the bedside table, picks up the packet of sleeping pills, and tips out the remaining blister pack, together with a folded instruction leaflet, which he unfurls and reads out of boredom*) "Warning: May cause drowsiness". Terrific. (*He crumples the instructions and takes out the remaining pill*) Goodnight, sweet prince, and flights of angels sing thee to thy rest.

He swallows the pill, swilling it down with a swig of gin, and switches off the bedside lamp to leave the stage in total darkness. A few moments later, a carriage clock strikes four am. Gentle moonlight illuminates a large window on the back wall. It is dressed only with net curtain. Wind begins to whistle loudly outside. Suddenly the window bursts open, as if blown inwards by the wind. The noise wakes Edward, who groggily gets up, shuts the window and collapses back onto the bed. Seconds later, it opens again.

Edward Bloody thing.

Irritably, he jumps up, this time slamming the window shut. There's a reaction he wasn't expecting - a sharp cry of pain from a female voice. Edward looks around, puzzled. Once again he gets back onto the bed, and once again he hears a strange, muffled voice, which appears to call his name. Petrified but intrigued, he walks warily towards the window, tension mounting, and reaches tentatively for the catch. Just as he touches it, there's a huge bang of thunder and flash of lightning, which sends him reeling backwards onto the floor, heart pounding. Floating outside the window, in a white shroud eerily lit by ultra-violet, is the ghost of his dead wife, Ruby. Edward is dumbstruck as the apparition slowly claws at the window, calling his name. Finally, he finds the courage to speak.

Edward What do you want with me?
Ruby Open the bloody window!

Edward feels compelled to obey. He opens the window and backs away. The apparition hoists up her smock and, in a rather unladylike manner, climbs through the window, closing it behind her. Edward slumps down in awe.

Ruby Not quite the entrance I had in mind. I tried the old walking through walls ploy and got stuck in the cavity. Not pleasant. I'm sure I've got fibreglass in my knickers. Still, here we are at last. Oh, come on, Edward - pull yourself together - you look like you've seen a ghost. Come on, stand up. Let me take a look at you.
Edward Ruby?
Ruby God, you look dreadful. I look better dead than you do alive.
Edward I'm dreaming. That's all it is. It's a dream.
Ruby You deal with this any way you like, sweetie, but deal with it. I haven't got time to prat about. Oh, do you mind? My shoes are killing me. (*She sits on the bed and takes off her shoes*) Oh, Heaven! Well, the nearest I'll get to it, anyway. So what are you doing living in this tip? What happened to our beautiful home? (*Edward is unable to respond, open-mouthed*) Edward? Speak to Ruby.
Edward It's a dream.
Ruby Oh, God. (*She looks around the room, spots a soda siphon, and squirts it directly into Edward's face to break his shock*) Wakey, wakey!

Edward It's a wet dream.

Ruby All right, it's a dream. Now talk to me.

Edward Are you real?

Ruby It depends what you mean by real.

Edward Do you exist? Or am I just going crazy?

Ruby Could be both.

Edward Can other people see you?

Ruby Of course not.

Edward How convenient. Can they hear you?

Ruby Come on, you know the rules.

Edward So you could just be a figment of my fevered imagination?

Ruby Perhaps.

Edward What was it Scrooge said? A slight disorder of the stomach affects the senses. "You may be an undigested bit of beef, a blot of mustard, a crumb of cheese, a fragment of underdone potato."

Ruby Or in your case, a dodgy curry.

Edward Ah, but hang on. You can move objects around the room.

Ruby Can I?

Edward You just picked up the soda siphon.

Ruby Yes, so I did.

Edward So if someone were to bump into you, they'd feel you.

Ruby Try it.

Edward thrusts his hand at Ruby. His arm apparently goes through her shroud and out the other side. He screams, withdrawing his hand quickly.

Edward Oh my God!

Ruby Weird isn't it? And yet I can touch you, and you can feel it.

She slaps him hard round the face, leaving him stunned.

Edward Yes, so I can.

Ruby Right, that's established the groundrules. I can touch you, you can't touch me, and no-one else can see me, or hear me. Unless, of course, I want them to.

Edward But...how?

Ruby Never mind how. Just concentrate on why.

Edward Why?

Ruby Because that's the way I want it. (*Spotting the gun, she picks it up and points it directly at her hand*) Does this work?

Edward No!!!

Ruby (*firing it inquisitively and examining her hand*) Oh, what a bore.

Edward (*tearing it from her*) It's a stage prop. Leave it alone.

Ruby All right, don't get tense.

Edward Look, I'm fed up with this dream now. Please, go away. Leave me alone.

Ruby Don't be pathetic.

Edward I'm going to close my eyes and count to three. (*He does, and starts counting*) One...

Ruby It'll end in tears.

Edward Two...

Alex, wearing pyjamas, bursts dramatically into the room and sees Edward, who is standing holding the gun, eyes tightly closed, looking as if he is counting down to a suicide.

Edward Three!

Alex No!!!!!

Alex leaps dramatically on Edward and flattens him onto the bed. Both men are screaming and wrestling maniacally, as Alex tries to take the gun from Edward, and Edward instinctively defends himself, unaware why he has been attacked and, initially, by whom. Edward finally manages to get Alex in a restraining necklock.

Edward Alex! What the hell are you doing?

Alex I heard a gunshot!

Edward It went off accidentally!

Alex Well how the hell am I supposed to know that? I thought you'd killed yourself!

Edward It's not even a real gun! You said so!

Alex All right, all right, let's just calm down. Let go.

Edward You let go.

Alex I'll let go when you let go.

Edward I've let go.

Alex All right, I'm letting go.

Ruby Well, well, well, Alexander. Still leaping on men in your pyjamas, I see.

Alex I've let go.

Edward Alex?

Alex What?

Edward Did you...hear anything then?

Alex (*disinterested - rubbing his neck*) Like what?

Edward Can you...see anybody else, in this room?
Alex Anybody else?
Ruby I've told you, he can't see me.
Edward You can't see a...woman, standing...somewhere?
Alex Like where?
Edward Like...there?
Alex (*suspiciously*) Can you?
Edward No.
Alex Are you sure?
Edward Positive. I just wondered if you could.
Alex Edward, I'm not leaving you alone tonight.
Ruby He says that to all the men.
Edward One of us is dreaming this.
Alex I hope it's me.
Ruby Can you get rid of him now? We've got work to do.
Edward Work?
Ruby Well I'm not here on holiday.
Alex What do you mean, work?
Edward Ah! So you heard her!
Alex Heard who?
Edward You heard her say work.
Alex You said work.
Edward No, she said it!
Ruby Just get rid him of him, Edward, before he calls an ambulance.
Alex Edward, I think you need help.
Edward I don't **need** a bloody ambulance.
Alex I never said you did.
Edward No, but she did.
Alex Edward!

Alex slaps Edward to bring him out of his hysteria.

Edward Ow! That hurt!

Edward, shocked, slaps him back.

Alex Stop it!
Edward You stop it!
Alex I'm trying to help you! (*He slaps him again*)

Edward I don't need your help! (*He slaps him back again*)
Alex All right! All right! Calm down! No more slapping.
Edward You started it.
Alex Edward, who is this...she?
Ruby You're making a mess of this. Just boot him out, now!
Edward I can't!
Alex You can't what?
Edward What?
Alex You can't say who she is?
Ruby Edward!
Alex Edward!
Edward One at a time!
Alex All right. You first.
Ruby Just repeat after me. Alex, I'm just tired, that's all.
Edward Alex, I'm just tired, that's all.
Ruby I've had a nasty dream.
Edward I've had a nasty dream.
Ruby I'd like you to go now, so I can get some rest.
Edward I'd like you to go now, so I can get some rest.
Alex Oh. Are you sure you're all right?
Ruby Quite sure.
Edward Quite sure.
Ruby Now show him the door.
Edward Now show him the door.
Alex Show who the door?
Ruby (*screaming impatiently at Alex*) Get out!!
Edward He can't hear you.
Alex Who can't hear me?
Edward She'd like you to leave, Alex.
Alex All right. I'm going.
Edward He's going.
Alex First thing in the morning, I want you to see a doctor.
Ruby Say goodnight, Alex.
Edward Goodnight, Alex.
Alex I'll see you in the morning.

Alex exits warily.

Ruby He hasn't changed.

A Flying Ducks Publication

Edward He's a good friend.

Ruby Yes. Good-looking chap, too. Pity he's gay.

Edward I'm sure he wouldn't see it that way.

Ruby Meaning?

Edward We weren't exactly a great advert for heterosexuality, were we?

Ruby Oh, I don't know. We had our moments.

Edward Did we?

Ruby At least it was never dull.

Edward Yes, I'll grant you that.

Ruby I'll bet there were times you despised me.

Edward Yes.

Ruby Go on, admit it!

Edward I just did.

Ruby Oh. Right. Well, that's all behind us now. So?

Edward So what?

Ruby Pleased to see me?

Edward Delirious. Yes, that's probably it. I'm delirious. I've got the flu.

Ruby Cheer up, sweetie. It's not every man can claim his wife has experienced a second coming. God knows the first is usually a challenge.

Edward Well, I wouldn't know. I haven't exactly been at my sexual peak for a while.

Ruby Oh, yes. How is the undercarriage by the way, still glittering?

Edward The last piece fell off on Monday.

Ruby Oh, better than expected. I thought it might put you out of action for a month or two, but a whole year!

Edward You were very thorough.

Ruby And very artistic, don't you think? Did you like the red cherry on the end?

Edward Dare I ask why?

Ruby Just trying to help out. You obviously thought your willy was a bit of a pop star, I just made it look the part.

Edward I was in agony.

Ruby You should just be grateful I'm an understanding sort of wife. My initial reaction was to chop it off and glue it to your brow.

Edward Are you going to tell me why?

Ruby Oh, I think you know why.

Edward Try me.

Ruby Were you ever unfaithful to me, Edward?

Edward No.

Ruby No?

Edward Not really.

Ruby From "No" to "Not really". Your denial is getting more surreal by the second.

Edward Here I am discussing adultery with a ghost, and you talk to me about surreal?

Ruby Yes or no, sweetie.

Edward I've forgotten the question.

Ruby Were you ever unfaithful to me?

Edward It depends how you define unfaithful.

Ruby Having sex with other women.

Edward In that case, I suppose I was.

Ruby So how do *you* define unfaithful?

Edward Wanting to have sex with other women.

Ruby In that case, every man in Britain is unfaithful.

Edward Good. That makes me feel less guilty.

Ruby So what are you saying - you had sex with other women but didn't want to?

Edward Yes. No. Don't know.

Ruby And what's that? A multiple choice answer?

Edward All I'm saying...I don't know what I'm saying. Look, I'm sitting up in the middle of the night having a conversation with a dead woman. You want me to be rational? I'm clearly insane, drunk, sleepwalking or feverish. What do you want from me?

Ruby All right, calm down. We're wasting time. I'll get to the point.

Edward Oh, so there's a point!

Ruby Damn right there's a point. Now listen carefully, I've got a little speech prepared. This is a big moment for me. Don't spoil it by interrupting. Ready? Oh, by the way, just for the purposes of the exercise, pretend that you loved me. Huge imaginative leap, I know, but if you can believe in ghosts, what the hell. Right, here we go. (*She assumes an imposing voice, and the wind begins to whistle ominously*)

> I am thy wife's spirit;
> Doom'd for a certain term to walk the night,
> And, for the day, confin'd to waste in fires
> Till the foul crimes done in my days of nature
> Are burnt and purg'd away. But that I am forbid
> To tell the secrets of my prison house,
> I could a tale unfold whose lightest word
> Would harrow up thy soul; freeze thy young blood;
> Make thy two eyes, like stars, start from their spheres;
> Thy knotted and combinéd locks to part,

> And each particular hair to stand on end,
> Like quills upon the fretful porpentine;
> But this eternal blazon must not be
> To ears of flesh and blood. List, list, O, list!
> If thou didst ever thy dear wife love...

Edward Oh, God!

Ruby Revenge her foul and most unnatural...

Edward Murder?

Ruby I told you not to interrupt!

Edward Sorry.

Ruby Murder most foul, as in the best it is;
> But this most foul, strange, and unnatural.

Terrific isn't it? What a great line. "Murder most foul". That's like the ghostie equivalent of "Follow that cab!" I know ghosts that would die to say that line.

Edward You were murdered?

Ruby Yep. As sure as I'm standing here.

Edward But I thought you died from...

Ruby A lethal cocktail of naughty pills and booze. Yes, I know. I was at the inquest. Problem is, Edward my old sweetie pie, I didn't take the pills. At least, not voluntarily. They were planted in my drink.

Edward By who?

Ruby That's what I want you to find out.

Edward This is madness.

Ruby Thou this be madness, yet there is method in't.

Edward It's a dream, isn't it?

Ruby Is it?

Edward I'm dead really.

Ruby Make your mind up, sweetie. Are you mad, dreaming or dead?

Edward I tried to shoot myself today. Maybe I succeeded.

Ruby I wouldn't recommend it. It's hell down there.

Edward Down there? You mean you went...

Ruby Just an expression, sweetie. No actually I haven't been anywhere yet. Can't. Not until I've sorted this out. Limbo, that's what they call it.

Edward Limbo?

Ruby Just think of Manchester Airport.

Edward So, how come it took you so long to come back?

Ruby Admin, sweetie. You've no idea of the amount of paperwork it takes just to get back here for a short visit. It's a bit like trying to make an insurance claim. Talking of which...

A Flying Ducks Publication

Edward No, I didn't get a penny.

Ruby What? Nothing? My breasts alone had a write-off value of fifty grand.

Edward The insurance company wriggled out of it, as usual.

Ruby How?

Edward They claimed it could have been suicide.

Ruby Suicide? What evidence could they possibly have for suicide?

Edward The fact that you were married to me.

Ruby You can see their point, though, can't you. So, you're stony broke, are you?

Edward Near enough. I haven't written a thing since you died, you know. Not a word.

Ruby Oh, dear. Good job I'm no longer a materialist, isn't it? It's right what they say, by the way - you can't take it with you. (*She holds her head*) Uh-oh!

Edward What's the matter?

Ruby I've got to go.

Edward Go where?

Ruby I'm starting to feel a bit faint. He warned me about this.

Edward Who did?

Ruby The first time is always the shortest. I've got to go and re-charge my batteries.

Edward Ruby?

Ruby Don't worry. I'll be back.

Edward Ruby!

Ruby The glow-worm shows the matin to be near,
And 'gins to pale his uneffectual fire
Adieu, adieu! Edward, remember me!

Ruby opens the window and slowly exits the way she came as she recites her final words, accompanied by the howling wind. The lights fade, first to ultra violet, showing Ruby as an eerie spectre, then to black. The wind dies down and gives way to twittering birds. Daylight streams through the window to reveal Edward asleep awkwardly on the bed. He tosses and turns on the bed, then suddenly sits bolt upright with a start, as if reacting to a bad dream. He looks around the room slowly, clearly bewildered. He gets up and cautiously examines the window. There's a knock on the door, which makes him jump out of his skin. Alex pops his head round the door.

Alex Only me.

Edward Oh, Alex. Come in.

Alex How are you feeling?

Edward All right, I think. I've had the weirdest night.

Alex I know. You told me.

Edward Did I?

Alex Nasty dreams.

Edward You think so?

Alex It's stress. Plays havoc with the mind. Sit on the bed. Open your mouth.

Edward Why?

Alex Just want to pop something under your tongue.

Edward This is no time to try and convert me, Alex.

Alex Don't be cheeky. Come on, be a good patient. (*He puts a thermometer in his mouth. Edward mutters something unintelligible*) It's rude to speak with your mouth full. All my friends know that. There now, let's see.

Edward Will I live?

Alex For the time being. At least until tonight. You haven't forgotten, have you?

Edward Glenda.

Alex She's a...

Edward Great girl, I know.

Alex Now, is there anything you need?

Edward I don't think so.

Alex Plain, ribbed, banana flavour, chocolate...

Edward Alex! I haven't even met the woman.

Alex I'll slip you a packet under the door, just in case.

Edward You will not!

Alex Can't be too careful.

Edward Alex, I am not having sex with this woman on our first date!

Alex Are you sure?

Edward I'm positive.

Alex I think she'll be relieved. I'll ring her and tell her.

Edward Alex! Get out!

Alex Just trying to help.

Edward Out!

Alex exits. Edward continues staring suspiciously around the room, before finally plucking up courage to call out.

Edward Ruby? Ruby? What am I doing? I'm talking to myself, that's what I'm doing. I'm going mad, that's what I'm doing. Are you? Yes I am actually. Oh, jolly good. A dream. Yes. That's what it was. A bad dream.

The lights fade to end the scene. As they fade back up, it is evening, and Edward is making a rather frantic and pathetic attempt to tidy his room. He starts by making the bed, finding and removing empty gin bottles from under the bedclothes as he goes. There is a waste bin, but it is bulging beyond its capacity. So the bottles make their way from inside the bed to under it. Also under the bedclothes he finds an old Chinese takeaway carton, which he hides under the rug - stamping it down to flatten the bulge. Finally, he looks around for somewhere to hide a discarded pair of underpants, and settles for dropping them out of the window. A few seconds later there's a distant screech of tyres from the street down below. There's a knock on the door. Edward checks his watch, then has a final glance around the room. He approaches the door and is about to open it when he does a sudden double-take on something he has spotted on the floor. Ruby's shoes. He picks them up and stares, trying to take in the awesome fact that her appearance was not a dream.

Edward My God. (*The door is knocked again*) Ruby?

In a daze, still holding the shoes, he opens it. Glenda - an attractive lady - is waiting nervously behind the door.

Glenda Hello.
Edward Can I help you?
Glenda If you're not expecting me, I'm going to die with embarrassment.
Edward You're Glenda.
Glenda Yes.
Edward (*surprised that she is attractive*) **You're** Glenda?
Glenda I'd better go.
Edward No, no! No, please. I'm sorry. Come in. Take a coat. Let me have your seat.

Glenda removes her coat, then notices as she goes to hand it over that Edward is holding a pair of lady's shoes.

Glenda Oh.
Edward Ah. Erm...(*darting a glance at her feet*) I see you've brought your own.
Glenda Yes.
Edward You won't be needing these then.
Glenda No.
Edward Right.
Glenda Nice thought, though.
Edward Coat.

He takes her coat, and dumps it unceremoniously on the bed.

Glenda Alex tells me you're a playwright.

Edward Oh, he's exaggerating.

Glenda But you do write plays.

Edward I used to. I haven't written anything since...(*he glances at the shoes in his hand, then quickly tosses them out of the window. Again we hear a distant tyre screech from below*)...for a while now. What about you?

Glenda I do a bit of acting, when I can.

Edward Of course. That's how you know Alex.

Glenda Not really. We met through my husband, actually. Well, ex-husband. We're divorced.

Edward I'm sorry.

Glenda It's all right. I don't mind talking about it. My psychiatrist says I should talk about it as often as possible.

Edward You have a psychiatrist?

Glenda Don't you?

Edward Not yet.

Glenda He had an affair.

Edward Your psychiatrist?

Glenda My husband.

Edward I see.

Glenda Alex helped me through the worst of it.

Edward He's a good chap, Alex.

Glenda Least he could do, really. It was Alex that my husband had the affair with.

Edward Ah.

Glenda I think he felt a bit guilty.

Edward Yes. I can see that. No wonder he was so keen to get us together.

Glenda It's not good for your self-confidence, when your husband leaves you for another man.

Edward No. Well, at least it was a gay man.

Glenda Sorry?

Edward Well, I thought it would have been worse still if...no, nothing. Erm, would you like a drink?

Glenda Er, no thanks, I don't.

Edward Don't what?

Glenda Drink. Well, not alcohol anyway. I'll have something else.

Edward What else is there?

Glenda Have you got a lime and lemon?

Edward I'm not with you.

Glenda Oh, look, just to be sociable, I'll try a teeny weency sherry.

Edward Oh, sherry. No, sorry. I could go out and get some...

Glenda No really, it doesn't matter.

Alex What about a gin and tonic - that's a lady's drink.

Glenda Never tried it.

Edward Never tried...you'll love it, trust me.

Glenda Oh, all right then. If you insist.

Edward I do. Now then, gin....gin...keep your fingers crossed...(*he opens the wardrobe*) You're in luck.

Glenda So I see.

Edward I like to keep some in. It's a bit of a trek to the off-licence.

Glenda Where do you keep your clothes?

Edward In the drinks cabinet. I don't have many. (*He hands her a full bottle, and takes one himself*) There you go.

Glenda (*bemused*) Erm...have you got a glass?

Edward It's all right, I don't need one. Oh, for you! Sorry, yes, a glass, of course. (*He looks around in a state of mild panic*) Won't be a second.

He dives out, leaving Glenda standing rather uncomfortably holding the bottle. Her eye is taken by a photograph of Ruby. She picks it up, but then the window is apparently blown open again by a freak wind. She is trying to shut it as Edward enters. He has a plastic pint glass in his hand, which he immediately puts down on the floor in order to close the window.

Edward Here, let me. I think the catch is a bit faulty. There.

Glenda Thanks. (*An uneasy pause*) Did you manage to get one?

Edward Get one?

Glenda Glass.

Edward Oh, glass, yes. I'm sure I had one. Excuse me.

Unable to find the original glass, he exits again. Glenda takes another look at the photograph, but replaces it hurriedly as Edward re-enters with another pint glass.

Edward Glass! (*He hands her the pint glass, immediately kicks over the other one on the floor, and hands her that as well*) Two glasses.

Glenda One's fine, thanks.

Edward Right. One for me then. Sorry about that. I'm a bit short of crockery and stuff. Most of it got broken at my last house.

Glenda Oh, when you moved.
Edward No, before I moved.
Glenda (*referring to the photograph*) Was this your wife?
Edward Yes.
Glenda Alex told me all about it. I'm sorry.
Edward Don't be. It wasn't your fault. At least I assume it wasn't.
Glenda No. Are you as nervous as I am?
Edward I don't know. How nervous are you?
Glenda More nervous than you think I am.
Edward You don't know how nervous I think you are.
Glenda Have you erm..had many girlfriends?
Edward Not since my wife died.
Glenda You had girlfriends before your wife died?
Edward No, I just meant - let me pour that drink for you.

He takes the bottle and glass and goes to the small table in the corner of the room to pour out a large gin. At that moment Ruby appears beside Glenda, who, of course, does not see or hear her.

Ruby You're not taking **this** to bed tonight, are you?
Edward (*his back to her*) What was that?
Glenda What?
Edward Did you say something?
Glenda No.
Edward Sorry. Right, er...gin. (*He looks around for tonic, but patently hasn't got any, so he shiftily grabs the gin bottle again and tops it up with that*) And tonic. (*Turning and offering the drink*) Your drink. (*He sees Ruby standing behind Glenda and instantly drops the glass on the floor in shock. He tries to cover his panic*) Is on the floor. I'll pour you another.
Glenda Oh. Are you sure?
Edward Positive. Plastic glasses. No problem.

Ruby glides alongside Edward, who picks up the glass and turns back to the table, still in a state of shock.

Ruby I said I trust you're not taking that moth-eaten specimen to bed tonight.
Edward (*in a manic whisper*) Go away!
Ruby Trying to get her tipsy, are we?
Edward I am merely trying to be sociable.

Ruby That's not a drink, it's an anaesthetic.
Glenda Sorry?
Edward What?
Glenda I thought you said something.
Edward No, no. Just muttering to myself.
Ruby She has all the personality of a trainee accountant. I've seen more life in a corpse.
Edward Will you please go away?
Ruby Get rid of her. You've got work to do.
Edward I can't. I promised Alex.
Ruby If you don't get rid of her, I will.
Edward Will you please disappear?
Ruby Disappear? Yes, all right. But I'll be around.

She exits. Edward turns with the glass in his hand.

Edward There. Ice and lemon?
Glenda Please.
Edward I haven't got any.
Glenda Oh, fine. Why did you ask?
Edward You might have said no.
Glenda Oh.
Edward There you go.
Glenda Thanks.

Just as he goes to hand Glenda the drink, an invisible force causes Edward to wrestle momentarily to control the movement of the glass.

Edward Stop it!
Glenda Stop what?

The movement seems to have stopped.

Edward Nothing.

He then calmly chucks the contents of the glass into her face.

Glenda Why did you do that?
Edward Why did I do that. Well, the thing is, Glenda, I have a sort of a nervous

twitch...thing, which makes me twitch, nervously, whenever I get nervous, over something. You see, whenever I'm with a woman, my arms and legs start doing things on their own.

Glenda That could get you into trouble.

Edward It often does.

Glenda Do I make you nervous?

Edward Not particularly.

At that moment, the picture on the wall behind Glenda (which is painted onto stretched rubber) is distended by Ruby's face pressing into it from behind. Edward jumps out of his skin and screams, causing Glenda to follow suit. She drops to her knees and covers her head with her hands.

Edward Sorry, sorry. My fault. I was, erm...look, the truth is, I've got this trapped nerve in my neck, and sometimes it just...golly that was a bad one. Are you all right. I'm so sorry.

Glenda I'm all right. You just scared me a little, that's all.

Edward I'm sorry.

Glenda It's all right. Trapped nerve?

Edward Yes.

Glenda It sounds painful.

Edward Yes. Can be.

Glenda How did it happen?

Edward Car accident. I was in a car, and it had...er...

Glenda An accident?

Edward Yes. That's it. Look, I'm sorry, we're getting off on the wrong foot. Why don't you sit down, and I'll have one last go at getting you this drink.

Glenda Right. Okay. Erm...where?

Edward Yes. Good point. I'm afraid that's why they call it a bedsit.

Glenda You want me to sit on the bed?

Edward Sorry.

Glenda That's okay.

Edward I'll get you another drink. It's all right. You'll be quite safe on there.

He goes to get another drink. She goes to sit down. The bed slides away from under her, and she lands with a bump on the floor, bewildered and screaming.

Edward That wasn't me! That was not me! Okay, okay. Look. Some pretty weird things are happening in this house, and you deserve to know the truth.

Glenda So?
Edward So here it is. The fact is, I haven't got a trapped nerve in my neck, okay?
Glenda Go on.
Edward There's actually a far more straightforward explanation.
Glenda I'm all ears.
Edward The fact is, my dead wife's ghost is in the room with us.
Glenda Thank you for a wonderful evening.
Edward No, it's true, and she gets a bit jealous, as you might expect, and so she's trying to get rid of you. And that's the truth.
Glenda I think I'd better be going.
Edward Glenda, I don't want you to go.
Glenda I'm sorry, Edward, you're not my type.
Edward What do you mean - not your type?
Glenda I'm not fussy, I just like sane people.

Edward starts ranting and virtually pins the petrified Glenda to the door.

Edward No, please, you can't go - look, I don't want her to win, I'm not going to let you win! Do you hear me? She is not going to spoil our evening. Look, I'll be honest with you, I didn't want you to come here tonight, but now you have and, well, I quite like you. And she is not...she is not going to do this to me! Glenda, please!

Glenda, wide-eyed, stands for a moment considering his plea, and her next move.

Glenda I can see her!
Edward Where?
Glenda Over there!

Edward spins round, and Glenda takes her chance to dive out through the door. Edward calls after her.

Edward Glenda! Come back! Please! Well that's terrific. Thanks a bunch.

Ruby re-appears.

Ruby She wasn't your type.
Edward She was just my type. She was paranoid, totally lacking in self-confidence and severely depressed. We would have got on just fine.

Ruby A tee-totaller!

Edward Only because you wouldn't let me get the drink in her mouth!

Ruby You were trying to seduce her.

Edward I was trying to be pleasant.

Ruby She was a dormouse.

Edward I like dormice. Dormice don't play with superglue.

Ruby You're just confused.

Edward And you're just jealous.

Ruby Jealous? Of what?

Edward Because she was everything you're not.

Ruby Such as?

Edward She was...what am I doing? I don't have to justify my girlfriends to you.

Ruby Just tell me one good thing about her, go on - just one redeeming feature.

Edward Well, she was alive for a start.

Ruby That's below the belt.

Edward I'll tell you what's below the belt - one set of extremely sensitive genitalia - that's what's below the belt.

Ruby Oh, not that old chestnut again.

Edward I happen to be rather fond of my old chestnuts.

Ruby Rather too fond if you ask me.

Edward I could have been scarred for life.

Ruby And that's all the thanks I get?

Edward Thanks?

Ruby For refurbishing your loins. It's not many wives who could keep their husbands faithful in such a decorative and creative way. You should be grateful.

Edward Well, thank you!

Ruby You're welcome.

Edward You've ruined my evening. No, sorry, correction, you've ruined my life.

Ruby Well just be grateful you've still got a life left to ruin. I no longer have that choice!

Edward's rage is defused by Ruby's final outburst, which is uncharacteristically emotional, and leaves her sobbing.

Edward I'm sorry.

Ruby Forget it. What are you staring at?

Edward I erm...I've never seen you cry before.

Ruby Horrible isn't it.

Edward No. It's not actually.

Edward goes to comfort her with a hug, but stops himself, unsure what would happen to his arms.

Ruby Have you got a cigarette?
Edward You don't smoke.
Ruby I do now.
Edward What for?
Ruby What do you mean, what for? I intend to enjoy myself, before it's too late.

Edward hands her a packet. She takes four at once and puts them in her mouth.

Edward You shouldn't do that.
Ruby What's it going to do? Damage my health?
Edward Do you drink as well?
Ruby Only spirits.
Edward Ho, ho.
Ruby Thank you. I've been waiting twelve months to use that line. I'll have a large
    G and T. And forget the T.

Edward shows her a large bottle from the wardrobe.

Edward Is that large enough for you?
Ruby It'll do for starters. (*She takes a swig*) Right, down to business. The coroner
    said that that combination of drink and pills would have put me out of the land of
    the living in less than two hours, right?
Edward I can't remember.
Ruby Oh, come on, sweetie, you were there.
Edward I was in shock.
Ruby Two hours, he said, tops. Now, cast your mind back to the last-night party.
    We've got the entire cast of Hamlet, six stage crew, hangers-on, groupies, a few
    press - about fifty people in total, right?
Edward Suppose so.
Ruby But, I shuffled off my mortal coil around four in the morning, so whoever put
    those pills in the glass must have been there until at least two am. Are you
    following me so far?
Edward I think so.
Ruby Right, now, let's narrow it down. The prat off the telly who played Hamlet,
    Jason Dildo or whatever his name was...

Edward Julian Dando.

Ruby That's him. Now, he graced us with his presence for, what, ten minutes, while the photographers were around, then he buggered off in his limo, right?

Edward Right.

Ruby Now, I reckon most of the hangers-on and bit parts left on the coach around eleven. That left all the normal hard-core revellers - me, you, Hedley, Howard, Frances, erm, who was that dreadful woman who did the make-up?

Edward Angela.

Ruby Angela, right.

Edward No, no - Angela left quite early.

Ruby Did she?

Edward Yes, don't you remember? You called her a titless wonder and she stormed out.

Ruby Good motive.

Edward But no opportunity. I'm sure she was gone before midnight. I remember because she made some remark about going before your face turned back into a pumpkin.

Ruby Never did like that girl. All right then, so that leaves Hedley, Howard, Frances...

Edward Hannah.

Ruby Who's Hannah?

Edward The one you said had more chins than a Chinese phone book.

Ruby Oh, yes. The scraggy little witch who was understudying Gertrude. Put her on the list.

Edward The one who criticised your technique.

Ruby Right at the top of the list.

Edward No, I don't think so. She was the one who found you. She looked really spooked. Either she's innocent, or she's a damn good actress.

Ruby She's innocent.

Edward Bitch.

Ruby What about Alex?

Edward Alex went home early. One of his migraines. Before eleven, I think.

Ruby Well that narrows it down quite nicely. Hedley, Howard, and Frances. Now, which one of those hated me enough to kill me?

Edward Hedley, Howard, and Frances.

Ruby You always did know how to flatter a girl. All right, so it's a one in three shot.

Edward One in four. You've forgotten one of the hangers-on.

Ruby Who?

Edward Me. How do you know I didn't murder you?

Ruby Because whoever did this had guts, and brains. Two commodities you're sadly lacking. Don't get me wrong, Edward, you're a good writer. But you lack the sort of brains that really matter in this world. Sense. Common sense. Financial sense. Dress sense.

Edward This is naive of me, I know. You always did insult me, but I thought when you died it might stop.

Ruby Hedley, Howard, Frances. All actors. Perfect.

Edward Perfect for what?

Ruby You're going to stage a little re-union.

Edward Oh, no. I haven't got the stomach for this.

Ruby Don't go chicken on me now, dear. I need you. I haven't got much time.

Edward Look, these people all loathe each other - they loathe me - what possible chance have I got of getting them all back together?

Ruby They're actors, Edward. Bad ones. And there's one thing that draws bad actors like a magnet. The promise of work. I want you to tell them you've written a play. Specially for them.

Edward But...they'll expect to see the script.

Ruby Then show them the script.

Edward I haven't got a script.

Ruby (*grabbing a sheet of paper and putting it into the typewriter*) Write one.

Edward I can't write one!

Ruby You're a writer!

Edward I was a writer! I haven't written anything in over a year.

Ruby Then it's about time you did.

Edward I can't.

Ruby I'll help you.

Edward I haven't got any ideas.

Ruby You have now. Write the play.

Edward What play?

Ruby A classic whodunit. Six characters. Five actors and a playwright. They'll be celebrating at a last night party. There's lots of bitchiness, rivalry. Then, at four in the morning, the wife of the playwright is found dead on the bed.

Edward Wait a minute. Is this leading where I think it's leading?

Ruby No-one suspects murder, of course, until the ghost of the dead wife comes back to spill the beans. She implores the writer to write a play mirroring the real murder, while the ghost carefully observes the protagonists for signs of guilt.

Edward (*his eyes widening with excitement, he moves towards his typewriter*) The play's the thing, wherein I'll catch the conscience of the king.

Ruby And we that have free souls, it touches us not. You could call it The

Mousetrap. No, a bit old hat. What about...

Edward (*typing*) Ghost Writer!

Ruby If you like. Just make sure the word Ghost is bigger than Writer. I demand top billing. Now, just as things are reaching a suitably gripping climax, I make my dramatic appearance in front of the guilty party, and put the willies up them good and proper.

Edward I thought you said no-one else could see you?

Ruby I'm an actress, darling. If it's essential to the plot, I'll do it.

Edward So who gets to play you at the beginning, before you die?

Ruby What do you mean?

Edward Well you can hardly play yourself. That would be giving the game away a bit wouldn't it.

Ruby Never thought of that.

Edward Glenda! She's an actress.

Ruby The dormouse?

Edward I'm sure she can play a rat.

Ruby Thanks, sweetie. Well, I suppose her figure's not bad. She'll need plenty of firm direction.

Edward I'll see to that.

Ruby Yes, I bet you will. All right, dormouse it is. Though God knows how you'll ever get her back into this house.

Edward I'll think of something.

Ruby Better start handing out the invites. I really haven't got much time.

Edward You keep saying that. You haven't got much time.

Ruby It's true. I'm on what you might call a bit of a deadline.

Edward How long have you got?

Ruby Ah. There's the rub.

Edward Tell me.

Ruby Well, in order to get back here, I had to do a...bit of a deal.

Edward What sort of deal?

Ruby I had to sign a sort of...contract.

Edward Who with?

Ruby Just a chap.

Edward What sort of chap?

Ruby Just a chap I met.

Edward Does he have a name?

Ruby Erm...several names I believe.

Edward Try me.

Ruby Well, I only knew him as...

Edward Ruby?

Ruby (*reluctantly*) Nick.

Edward (*flatly*) Nick.

Ruby Yes.

Edward Nick what?

Ruby Just Nick.

Edward Is that his Christian name?

Ruby Oh, I doubt it.

Edward This wouldn't, by any chance, be Old Nick, would it?

Ruby Well, he was getting on a bit, yes.

Edward Oh, Ruby!

Ruby It's all right - he was a nice chap! Better the one you know, I say.

Edward Have you paid him?

Ruby Not yet.

Edward Then pull out. Pull out of the contract.

Ruby Not that simple, I'm afraid, sweetie. Once you take the goods, you have to pay up. It's sort of...direct debit.

Edward Terrific.

Ruby It was only a soul. He wasn't interested in anything else. He said I could keep the rest.

Edward What rest?

Ruby I don't know - sense of humour.

Edward Where you're going you're going to need a sense of humour.

Ruby Look, I got here didn't I? He delivered his part of the bargain.

Edward He conned you.

Ruby No, I conned him. I simply sold him something he probably already owned. Look, can we stop moralising and get on with this? This is important to me. It's all I've got left!

Edward I'm sorry.

Ruby (*producing a paper contract*) Now, according to the contract, I've only got three visits. I don't know how long each visit lasts - could be a minute, could be a year - except they get longer each time. But, as we now know, I'm already on number two. It's a bit like drowning. You float to the surface three times, and then...that's it.

Edward What's this? My name's in here!

Ruby Don't panic. It's just a formality. You're allowed one confidant - that's you - the only living person who can see me and hear me. Make sure you pick someone you can really trust, Nick said. I picked you. Flattered?

Edward Ironic, isn't it? I once asked you if you trusted me. And you said something about...

Ruby Over my dead body. I know. Well, here it is.

Edward snatches the contract from Ruby, who chases him around the room.

Ruby Hey! Some parts of that are private!

Edward Don't talk to me about private parts.

Ruby All right. Read it. See if I care.

Edward (*reading the contract*) I can't believe you signed this.

Ruby This is important to me, Edward.

Edward (*reading*) "Remuneration. In consideration of the sum of...one soul. Plus VAT"?

Ruby He's a bit of a joker. Look at the General Exclusions clause.

Edward (*reading*) Acts of God.

Ruby Yes. It's about all he can't cope with. Floods, war, civil insurrection are all a positive bonus.

Edward Sounds like a pleasant fellow.

Ruby Oh, he's all right. Bit misunderstood. I blame the parents. He was kicked out, you know, when he was just...

Edward All right, spare me the theology lesson.

Ruby Anyway. I don't think I can rely on divine intervention - not with my track record.

Edward No.

Ruby Oh, yes, the small print. Have a look at Clause Thirteen. How would you interpret that?

Edward Er..the party of the first part may, upon.....(*he mutters to himself*) Well I'm no lawyer, but I'd say it means that you can, in exceptional circumstances, allow yourself to be seen and heard by people other than the named confidant.

Ruby Right...

Edward But once you do...

Ruby That's the final act.

Edward Yes.

Ruby That's what I thought. A bit like a bee, stinging its victim.

Edward So, what...happens to you - when this is all over?

Ruby That's down to Nick. He said he'd look after me.

Edward I bet he did!

Ruby I think he felt a bit sorry for me. Cut off in my prime. And me such a good disciple. Anyway, before I signed the contract, he said he couldn't promise anything, but if all went well, he'd try and sort out something special for me.

Edward Special?

Ruby A surprise ending.

Edward Oh, Ruby!

Ruby Don't worry. I don't think he's really interested in me. I'm just a pawn. A delivery girl.

Edward Delivering what?

Ruby The main man. The one who poisoned me. He's got big plans for him! No, hopefully, when all this is over, he'll have no further use for me. I'll be like any out-of-work actor. I get to rest.

Edward I'm not sure I want that.

Ruby I want it.

Edward Are you certain?

Ruby Oh, yes. There's nothing more certain than death.

Edward I'm going to lose you twice.

Ruby I'm already dead, Edward.

Edward How can you say that? How can you stand there and claim to be dead?

Ruby Don't get taken in by my lively exterior. This is all an illusion. Just a way of making it make sense to you.

Edward But it doesn't make sense to me.

Ruby I know, it's tricky stuff. One day, you'll understand.

Edward But you can't be dead. It's just a technicality, right? I mean, you're talking. At times you almost seem to be enjoying yourself. You think, therefore you are.

Ruby No, **you** think, therefore I am.

Edward So what - now you're saying I'm imagining you?

Ruby Not exactly. No more than a television imagines pictures and sound. But without the television, there are no pictures, no sound - just a meaningless, invisible, inaudible signal.

Edward That almost made sense.

Ruby It's the best I can do. The full explanation would take a lifetime. And I haven't got...

Edward ...much time. All right.

Ruby Pick up the phone, Edward. Call the actors. Whatever else happens, make sure you get Hedley, Howard and Frances. One of them is a murderer.

Edward When?

Ruby Tomorrow night.

Edward Tomorrow night? But...

Ruby There's no more time. Tomorrow night. Bribe them if you have to.

Edward What with?

Ruby Insurance money. We're about to rule out suicide.

A Flying Ducks Publication

Edward But what about the play?
Ruby Ah, yes, the play. Here. Let me give you a hand.

She closes her eyes and meditates. Suddenly, the electric typewriter at which Edward is sitting bursts into life, printing out all by itself (a simple effect to achieve, using a pre-programmable typewriter). Edward draws back in awe, staring in amazement at the words materializing on the page. The lights fade as the page works its way up the carriage. End of Act One.

ACT TWO

Edward has crashed out asleep on the bed, clutching a large wad of papers. There's a knock on the door, which wakes him with a start, and Alex pops his head round the door.

Alex Are you ready for us, maestro?
Edward (*disorientated*) What?
Alex Your guests have arrived.
Edward What time is it?
Alex Ten past eight.
Edward Shit. I must have crashed out.
Alex I'm not surprised. Your little typewriter was clattering away all night. You must have worked like a man possessed.
Edward Yes. Yes, I did.
Alex So, do you need some time to freshen up, or are you going for the Bohemian writer look?
Edward What do you think?
Alex Mmm, at least drag a comb through your hair. These are sensitive creatures out there. Hang on to the stubble, though, it suits you. And I don't want to get too personal, but you've had the same clothes on for two days.
Edward Why don't you just buy an Action Man?
Alex One of us has to take a pride in your appearance.
Edward Just give me a few minutes.
Alex All right. I'll fix them up with a little drinkie. You're a bit short on variety. Back in a jiff.

He exits. Edward starts pacing the room nervously, looking for Ruby.

Edward Ruby? Ruby? Come on, Ruby. Don't desert me now. They're here. I can't go through with this on my own. Where the hell are you? (*He opens the window*) I'll leave it open for you.

Alex pops back in.

Alex Oh, forgot to mention. Howard's had to cry off at the last minute.
Edward What?
Alex Something to do with his mother-in-law's colostomy bag, I don't know - I didn't

want to go into details. Anyway, he says sorry he can't make it tonight, but count him in next time.

Edward But that's ruined everything!

Alex Don't panic, I'll read in for Howard. We'll soon get the gist.

Edward No, you don't understand. He's got to come!

Alex Calm down! Wow, you're tetchy. It's only a read-through, Edward. Hardly a matter of life and death.

He exits, leaving Edward looking extremely tense. He slumps down onto the bed.

Edward Damn!

This instantly causes Ruby, hiding under the bed, to scream, which in turn causes Edward to jump out of his skin. He pulls the bed aside to reveal Ruby on the floor.

Ruby Thanks. You frightened the life out of me.

Edward Where the hell have you been?

Ruby Disneyworld.

Edward What?

Ruby Thought I'd squeeze in a flying visit.

Edward Why?

Ruby Never went as a kid.

Edward Oh, fine! So I'm stuck here panicking and you're shaking hands with Mickey Mouse?

Ruby You were asleep.

Edward I don't believe this.

Ruby Look, don't start on me. It was my last chance for a dream holiday. Even that went horribly wrong. I ended up in bloody Paris.

Edward This is your crusade, Ruby. The least you can do is be here when they arrive.

Ruby I was, sweetie! This body materializing business is harder than it looks, you know. I've been stuck under the floorboards for two hours.

Edward Howard's not coming.

Ruby I've got fluff up my nose now.

Edward I said, Howard's not coming!

Ruby I know, I heard. You've got some disgusting things under your bed.

Edward It's a disaster.

Ruby You're telling me. Gin bottles. Fag packets.

Edward Ruby!

Ruby A dead mouse.

Edward We can't go through with this!

Ruby It was covered in maggots.

Edward How can we have a whodunit if one of the people that could have dunit ain't here?

Ruby Dead maggots. Even the maggots were covered in maggots.

Edward Ruby, listen to me!

Ruby Or was it a portion of fried rice?

Edward I'm calling it off!

Ruby Don't be stupid! We've still got two out of three, haven't we? There's still a good chance the murderer is here tonight. If it's Frances or Hedley, we'll soon know.

Edward And if it isn't?

Ruby Then we'll know it's Howard. Either way, the plan works. Underpants.

Edward What?

Ruby There's something rotten in the state of your underpants. I found a pair under the bed.

Edward Will you forget my underpants?

Ruby Not in a hurry. They were gross.

Another knock on the door, and Alex enters.

Alex Can we come in?

Edward Erm, yes. Please.

Alex Pray silence, for Queen Gerdrude, and King Claudius.

Frances and Hedley enter, followed nervously by Glenda. They are all carrying huge pint glass drinks. Frances and Hedley eye the attic room with a degree of disgust.

Edward Frances, you're looking lovelier than ever.

Ruby She started from a very low base.

Frances Oh, Edward, you're just saying that.

Ruby Course he is you silly cow.

Edward No, I mean it. You seem to get younger every year.

Ruby And we all know why, don't we. If she has any more face-lifts she'll be using her breasts as shoulderpads.

Edward Nice dress.

Frances Thank you.

Edward Magnificent shoulderpads.

A Flying Ducks Publication

Ruby Stop flirting.

Hedley How's it going, young man?

Edward *(distracted by Hedley's horrendous hairpiece)* Wigley! Er...Hedley, thanks for coming.

Hedley Always happy to help out a starving artist.

Ruby Patronising git. God, that wig gets worse every year. It's virtually orange.

Edward Glenda.

Glenda Edward.

Edward Welcome back.

Glenda Thank you.

Ruby Make sure she doesn't fall asleep in the teapot.

Edward I see you finally got a drink.

Glenda Yes, sherry.

Edward Alex, are you sure these drinks are large enough?

Alex Look, I'm not diving up and down those stairs every five minutes. They've got to last all night.

Edward Take it steady.

Glenda I will.

Ruby Look at you. Your eyes are on stalks.

Edward Excuse me. *(To Ruby, through gritted teeth)* Will you keep quiet?

Ruby You may as well wear a day-glo badge saying you want to roger the woman.

Edward There is nothing wrong with being pleasant. You should try it some time.

Ruby Look, sweetie, let's just get one thing straight. You stand about as much chance of getting your leg over the dormouse as I do of passing a medical. So do yourself a favour, concentrate on the job in hand.

Hedley *(looking around at the lack of furniture)* Where am I supposed to park my bottom?

Alex Don't look at me.

Edward Alex, could you get some chairs?

Alex We could just as easily do this in my lounge, you know.

Edward No, I prefer to stay on home ground, thanks.

Alex Suit yourself.

Alex exits.

Hedley You actually **live** here?

Edward Yes.

Hedley Christ.

Ruby *(she pulls up some of Frances' hair to take a close-up peek behind her ear)*

Come and take a look at this lot! It's like a kids' embroidery class!
Frances It is...an interesting room.

Frances, bemused, brushes her hair back down with her hand.

Edward It's just temporary.
Ruby So's this face.
Edward Alex was good enough to let me stay till I sorted myself out.
Ruby (*lifting her hair again*) If I was to unpick one of these stitches she'd go off like an inflatable life-raft.
Frances (*brushing it down again*) Lot of static in the air tonight.
Ruby It's probably Hedley's bri-nylon wig. It's a wonder he hasn't got balloons stuck to it.

Alex enters carrying two chairs.

Alex How many are there of us?
Edward Er, two, four, six.
Hedley Call me a stickler for detail, but I make it five.
Edward Er, two, four, five, sorry. Yes.
Ruby Steady, sweetie. Keep your wits about you.
Edward (*suddenly forgetting himself and snapping at Ruby*) It would help me concentrate if you didn't talk!

There's a sudden, hurt silence from Glenda, who was chatting quietly in the background to Frances, and assumes Edward's remark is aimed at her, as she is standing directly behind Ruby. Ruby glides out of the way.

Glenda (*hurt*) I'm sorry.
Alex Give us a hand, Hedley.
Hedley What for?
Alex (*exiting*) Get some chairs.
Hedley Oh. (*Following him out*) Haven't we got stagehands for that sort of thing?

Alex and Hedley have left the room.

Ruby I think you'd better apologize to the dormouse.
Edward I'm sorry, dormou...Glenda, I didn't mean you.
Glenda Yes you did.

Edward No I didn't.

Glenda You were staring right at me.

Edward I know, but...

Glenda I was only introducing myself to Frances.

Edward Look, don't ask me to explain.

Ruby Oh, go on, ask him to explain.

Edward (*to Ruby, who is momentarily standing directly between Edward and Frances*) Are you trying to make things worse?

Frances Don't start on me, darling! I never said a word!

Edward Excuse me, ladies. (*He follows Ruby into the corner of the room*) You're making this impossible for me!

Ruby This is my party, remember.

Edward You're supposed to be here as an observer!

Ruby I've waited a year for this moment, I intend to enjoy every minute of it.

Edward If you're not careful, you'll blow it. Just keep your mouth shut.

We tune into Frances and Glenda chatting in the opposite corner of the room.

Frances Yes, it's in the blood in our family. My husband was SM at the RSC for ten years. Had to pack it up though - RSI.

Glenda Sorry?

Frances Repetitive Strain Injury. Curtains.

Glenda Oh, dear.

Frances My son Ryan runs the I.T. department at the Arts Council. And my daughter Lucy's PA to the MD at ENO.

Glenda ENO?

Frances English National Opera. I thought you were in the bizz?

Edward (*moving alongside them*) She was. Had to pack it up. Bad case of RAI.

Frances RAI?

Edward Repetitive Acronym Injury. Ah, Alex!

Enter Alex, carrying two chairs, and Hedley, carrying one.

Alex Anyone care for a seat?

Hedley I thought I was being invited here as an actor, not some kind of bloody labourer.

Frances What would you do, Hedley, if you ever got offered a role that involved some sort of physical effort?

Hedley Haven't you ever heard of stand-ins?

Edward All right, grab a seat everybody, we'll make a start. (*They all settle down, and Edward paces nervously*)

Ruby Knock 'em dead, sweetie. Metaphorically, of course.

Edward Thanks. Er, thanks, first of all, for turning up. That's those of you that did, of course.

Ruby Stop waffling.

Edward Now, you all know why you're here.

Hedley Your new play.

Edward My new play, exactly, yes.

Frances We're all dying to hear about it, Edward.

Edward Thank you, Frances. Well...

Frances But first things first. (*Producing a filofax*) Let's get the dates sorted out. Things are getting pretty chock-a for me right now, as you might expect.

Ruby (*looking over her shoulder*) There's nothing in there!

Edward Oh, well, I hadn't really thought about production dates yet.

Frances Sorry, darling, but I've got to know. I'm not the easiest woman to pin down lately.

Ruby Not what I've heard.

Edward Well, I was thinking, sort of Autumn-time.

Frances (*sharp intake of breath*) Tricky. Might be able to squeeze you in.

Ruby Hang on, what's this?

Frances (*flicking through her diary*) Can I take it we'd be all through by October fifteenth?

Edward I suppose so.

Ruby (*squinting at the filofax*) Harley Street.

Frances Good. Only after that I'm going to be a bit tied up - there's something really big going down.

Ruby She's having her tits lifted again.

Edward All right, Frances, we could go for early Autumn. But aren't we jumping ahead a bit? You might not even like the play.

Hedley Too bloody right.

Edward Thank you, Hedley.

Hedley Just agreeing with you. Look, no offence, old chap...(*he takes a slurp of his drink, allowing Ruby to interject*)

Ruby Why do people always say that just before they offend you?

Hedley I mean, your last one did the business - fair enough - but there are no guarantees in this game - know what I mean? What if this one turns out to be a pile of steaming dog mess?

Frances Then you'll be perfectly cast in the lead.

Alex Well, perhaps instead of all this intense speculation, we could just get on and read the play?

Edward I thought a quick synopsis first.

Hedley We're all ears.

Edward Right, well, here goes.

Ruby Speak the speech, I pray you, as I pronounced it to you, trippingly on the tongue.

Edward It's a ghost story.

Frances A ghost story! That's novel.

Hedley What sort of ghost story? Scary? Funny?

Edward Well, it's got some scary bits, and some funny bits.

Hedley Are the scary bits funny, or the funny bits scary?

Frances Shut up, Hedley, let him explain.

Edward First of all, I must apologize again to Glenda.

Glenda It's all right, forget it.

Alex What's up?

Edward Well, as I explained to Glenda on the phone, when we last met I'm afraid I used her as a bit of a guinea pig. I tried out some of the ghost scenes on her, just to see how she'd react - didn't I, Glenda.

Glenda Yes, certainly scared me.

Edward Sorry, Glenda, that was a bit naughty of me.

Glenda Glad to help.

Ruby So that's how you got her here.

Hedley All right, so we've established it's a scary ghost story with some funny bits.

Edward It's really more of a whodunit.

Frances Ah, so one of us is a murderer.

Edward Quite probably.

Hedley Me, I suppose.

Edward Not necessarily.

Hedley I always get cast as the bloody villain.

Frances What do you expect, looking like that?

Hedley What the hell's that supposed to mean?

Frances Well, Hedley, how can I put this subtly?

Ruby Don't break the habit of a lifetime, darling.

Frances You're hardly in line to be the next James Bond, are you, darling?

Hedley Well that shows what you bloody know - darling. Actually I was shortlisted for Bond three years ago and turned the bugger down.

Frances No, darling, let's get the facts straight, shall we? First of all it was fifteen years ago, and you were booked to play a non-speaking extra in a street fight. They sacked you because you were so drunk you fell over before Bond had time to hit you.

Hedley (*melodramatically*) O, 'tis true, 'tis too true.

Ruby Oh, God. He's off.

Hedley How swift a lash that speech doth give my conscience!

Ruby I wouldn't mind if he'd get the words right, just once!

Glenda How did you know all that?

Frances In the bizz, darling. My uncle was cameraman on the shoot.

Hedley Alas! Alas!

Frances Oh, stick a sock in it, Hedley!

Ruby That's a good idea. (*She looks around for a sock*)

Alex I thought we were here to talk about Edward's play?

Hedley Frailty, thy name is that of woman...uuummph!

Unseen by the others, Ruby has found a disgusting old sock and stuffed it into Hedley's mouth. Totally bemused, he slowly pulls out the sock, and checks his drink.

Alex So, we've got a ghost story and a whodunit. Sounds good so far, Edward. Tell us more.

Edward It's about a writer. A playwright, actually.

Frances A bit like you.

Edward Indeed. A bit like me. And he's written a new play.

Alex A bit like you!

Edward A bit like me. And then, at a last night party at the theatre, his wife tragically dies from an overdose of booze and drugs. (*There's a stunned silence - even Hedley now turns his attention from the sock to Edward*) A bit like me, really.

Ruby That's wiped the grin off their faces. Right, let's see who looks the most rattled. Go on. You're doing wonderfully.

Alex (*getting up*) Edward, are you sure about this?

Edward Quite sure.

Ruby Deadpan. Both of them. Turn the screw a bit.

Edward Right, well, this is where it starts to get intriguing. A year later, the wife's ghost comes back to warn the writer that she was, in fact...

Ruby Here comes the crunch.

Hedley In fact what?

Ruby (*staring intently at Hedley and Frances*) Go on, go for it. I'm ready.

Edward That she was, in fact...

Alex (*standing apart from the rest*) Murdered.

Edward (*surprised*) Yes.

Alex Echoes of Hamlet.

Edward Indeed.

Alex Well, if you're going to rip off a play, may as well rip off a good'un.

Ruby Can't tell. They both look a bit edgy.

Hedley Look, I don't want to be a bore...

Frances Too late, Hedley.

Hedley Can't we just read the bloody play?

Edward All right. (*Handing out manuscripts*) Glenda, if you don't mind, I'd like you to play Ruby...

Frances Ruby?

Edward I haven't had time to come up with fictitious character names, I'm afraid. You're all playing under your own names for now. Except for Ruby, of course who, well, (*pretending to be choked with emotion*) can't be here tonight.

Ruby Oh, here we go. Eyes down in mock reverence.

Alex Tragic.

Ruby Isn't it just.

Frances Poor Ruby.

Ruby Dead, darling, but never poor.

Edward So, I thought Glenda could play her part, if you don't mind, Glenda?

Glenda I'd be honoured.

Ruby You're out of your depth, darling.

Edward And Alex, if you could play yourself...

Alex Second nature, darling.

Frances He said play yourself, Alex, not play with yourself.

Edward And also read Howard's parts. We'll start right from the top. (*Hedley is once again looking a little distracted*) Ready, Hedley?

Hedley Is this your sock?

Edward I think so. Where did you find it?

Hedley You don't want to know.

Edward I'll do the stage directions. (*He begins reading the stage notes, moving towards the light switch*) "The setting is Edward's scruffy bedsit room, which is an upstairs attic room within Alex's flat. The stage is black. (*He switches off the main lights, and moves in the darkness to sit on the packing case*) A shadowy figure is sat on a packing case at a small writing table. An anglepoise lamp is switched on (*he switches on the anglepoise*) eerily up-lighting the face of Edward, who stares into space with a look of grim foreboding. He begins to utter some famous words: *To be, or not to be, that is the question.*"

The anglepoise goes off to end the scene. The main lights come on to reveal the actors reading from their manuscripts. Glenda is playing Ruby's part.

Edward It's about a writer. A playwright, actually.

Frances A bit like you.

Edward Indeed. A bit like me. And he's written a new play.

Alex A bit like you!

Edward A bit like me. And then, at a last night party at the theatre, his wife tragically dies from an overdose of booze and drugs. (*There's a stunned silence*) A bit like me, really.

Glenda That's wiped the grin off their faces. Right, let's see who looks the most rattled. Go on. You're doing wonderfully.

Alex (*getting up*) Edward, are you sure about this?

Edward Quite sure.

Glenda Deadpan. Both of them. Turn the screw a bit.

Edward Now, this is where it starts to get intriguing. A year later, the wife's ghost comes back to warn the writer that she was, in fact...

Glenda Here comes the crunch.

Hedley In fact what?

Glenda (*staring intently at Hedley and Frances*) Go on, go for it. I'm ready.

Edward That she was, in fact...

Alex (*standing apart from the rest*) Murdered.

They close their manuscripts. There's a look of total bewilderment on all the actors' faces.

Edward End of Act One. Well?

Frances This is weird.

Alex Some of the text...it seemed...word for word.

Edward Divine inspiration.

Frances But how did you know...we were going to say all that stuff?

Edward I didn't. Until tonight.

Hedley What the bloody hell is this? Some sort of mass hypnosis?

Edward There are more things in heaven and earth, Hedley, than are dreamt of in your philosophy.

Glenda Well, it certainly sets up the second half nicely. I suppose this is where we all find out whodunit.

Edward Yes, I hope so.

Frances What do you mean, hope so?

Edward Well, truth is, I haven't quite finished writing the second act yet.

Glenda Oh, what a shame.

Edward I was hoping you could all help me.

Frances Help you?

Edward As characters in the plot, just like you did in the first half. We can knock some ideas about - discuss motivations - that sort of thing. It's quite a trendy way of writing these days.

Alex This is all hypothetical, of course.

Edward Of course. I ask you some searching questions. You tell me what you - or rather your characters - might think or do in the circumstances.

Glenda Sounds fascinating.

Edward Good. Well let's start with you, Frances.

Frances Me? Why me?

Edward Because you've got the best motive for murder.

Frances Have I?

Edward I mean your character.

Frances Hypothetically.

Edward Of course.

Frances Okay, what's my motivation?

Edward You hated Ruby.

Frances Did I?

Edward I think so.

Frances Why?

Edward Because she always got the leading roles.

Frances Not true.

Ruby Oh, come on!

Frances I hated Ruby generally, not for any specific reason.

Ruby Bless her.

Alex Can I remind you, Edward, that no-one hated Ruby more than you did.

Hedley Oh I dunno. I bet I did.

Alex You hated Ruby too?

Hedley Good Lord, yes. (*Standing*) Look, I'm sorry if this all comes as a bit of a shock to you, Edward, old fruit, but I never could stomach your wife.

Ruby I bet you wouldn't say that to her face.

Hedley And what's more, I'd say it to her face.

Ruby Let me pull his wig off.

Hedley I'm not one to speak ill of the dead or anything, but she was a selfish, two-faced, obnoxious, whining old crone. Hypo-bloody-thetically, of course.

Edward goes to strike Hedley, but is restrained by Alex.

A Flying Ducks Publication

Alex Hey! Stop that.

Ruby Allow me. (*Ruby gives Hedley a sharp little knee in the groin, and he collapses, perplexed, back into his seat*) A hit, a very palpable hit.

Alex Hedley's right, you know.

Edward Et tu, Alex?

Alex Yes, the truth hurts, doesn't it.

Hedley It certainly bloody does.

Glenda Are you all right?

Hedley Touch of indigestion.

Frances So you hated Ruby too, did you, Hedley?

Hedley Said so, haven't I?

Frances Is that why you slept with her?

Ruby What?

Edward What?

Hedley What?

Frances That night, at the party.

Hedley Did I?

Ruby This is nonsense.

Frances I walked in on you in the props room, while you were making the beast with two backs and orange hair.

Edward (*to Ruby, who is, for a moment, directly in front of Frances*) You had sex with Hedley?

Frances (*as Ruby glides out of the way*) Not me, dear, Ruby. Pay attention.

Ruby She's just stirring it. I wouldn't touch Hedley with a vermin stick.

Edward (*to Frances, after a short deliberation*) I don't believe you.

Frances Suit yourself.

Ruby Thank you, Edward.

Edward Don't mention it.

Glenda (*who is now getting quite drunk on her sherry*) Don't mention what?

Edward Nothing.

Frances What's she hiding?

Glenda I'm not hiding anything.

Frances Then why did he tell you not to mention it?

Glenda I don't know what he's talking about!

Edward Look, if it makes you feel better, just mention it.

Glenda Mention what?

Edward Whatever you like.

Glenda I haven't got anything to mention. I wasn't even there!

Hedley I don't remember sleeping with her.
Ruby You see?
Frances No, you wouldn't. Apparently it's a very forgettable experience.
Ruby Bitch!
Frances At least, that's what most of the men around here say.
Ruby Just one tug of this twine, and her face hits the carpet.
Hedley Well all I can say is, I must have been very drunk.
Frances I think we can take that for granted, don't you?
Hedley What's that supposed to mean?
Frances Well you do have a wee bit of a drink problem, don't you, Hedley.
Hedley Are you saying I'm an alcoholic?
Frances Well, let's face it, darling, you didn't get that nose by sipping milk, did you?
Hedley What's wrong with my nose?
Frances Darling, it's got varicose veins.
Edward All right, let's get back to the point.
Hedley Now hold on. This woman is implying I'm a drunk.
Frances No, I'm not implying it, Hedley, I'm just stating it categorically.
Hedley That's a damned slur.
Frances So was that.
Hedley The lady protests too much, methinks.
Frances The gentleman drinks too much, methinks.
Hedley Get thee to a nunnery.
Frances Get thee to a brewery.
Hedley I've a good mind to give you a bloody good hiding.
Frances Don't be ridiculous Hedley, that would involve getting up off your chair. You're far too lazy and far too pissed.
Edward This is getting out of hand.
Frances Agreed. And unfortunately it proves nothing. Sorry, Edward, but sleeping with Ruby doesn't exactly make Hedley unique. Name me a man in stripping distance who didn't.
Ruby Excuse me!
Edward Excuse me!
Alex Excuse me!
Frances All right, Alex - you're off the hook. The rest of you get back in line.
Ruby This is when you really find out who your true friends are.
Edward That's my wife you're talking about!
Alex Come on, Frances. The woman's gone. Let's show some respect.
Frances Oh, you mean like he did when she was alive.
Edward She was my wife. We were entitled to get on badly.

Frances Perhaps if you'd looked after her more in the first place she might still be
     alive.

Edward That's despicable!

Ruby (*she angrily brandishes a gin bottle behind Frances' head, seen only by a
     bemused Hedley and Glenda*) Just say the word, Edward.

Frances You did tell her about us, I take it?

Edward Us?

Frances Us, yes. Me and you.

Ruby (*dropping the bottle into Hedley's lap, causing him a minor relapse*) What does
     she mean - us?

Edward (*to Ruby*) I don't know.

Frances You don't know? Surely you know if you told her or not?

Ruby Told me what?

Frances Did she, or did she not, know that we were lovers?

Ruby What?

Edward Erm, well, she didn't.

Frances Aha!

Edward But...

Ruby She does now.

Edward She does now. Beam me up, Scottie.

Hedley (*dumbfounded, preoccupied with the gin bottle*) Did anybody see that?

Alex You....and Frances?

Edward I paid for that mistake, believe me.

Hedley The gin bottle went up in the air. Did you see it?

Glenda I think I saw it.

Ruby You went to bed with this patchwork quilt?

Edward (*to Ruby*) I'm sorry.

Frances What for?

Edward (*turning to Frances*) I'm sorry I slept with you.

Frances Bit late now, darling. No good complaining to the chef after you've licked
     the bowl clean.

Ruby What a delightful image.

Glenda (*heavily slurring*) Listen everybody, listen up. Now, I don't know how
     important this is, in the scheme of things, but Hedley and I, and Hedley, both think
     that we just saw a gin bottle floating in the air.

Alex Don't worry about it, Glenda. That sort of thing tends to happen after a pint of
     sherry.

Hedley I'm telling you, the bloody gin bottle was floating.

Frances Well, you can't knock the credibility of the witnesses. Let's call in the paranormal scientists.

Alex I hope neither of you two are thinking of operating any heavy machinery later.

Edward This is getting us nowhere. Look, let's accept for a moment that you all had a good motive to kill Ruby. The question is, who had the opportunity?

Frances The real question is, who mixed Ruby's last drink?

Edward Well, yes.

Frances And the answer is, I did.

Alex You?

Frances Yes.

Alex Are you actually admitting that you made Ruby's last drink?

Frances Yes.

Edward And handed it to her?

Frances Yes.

Edward What was in it?

Frances As I recall, it was a G and T, with the emphasis heavily on the G.

Edward And a bucket-load of barbiturates.

Frances As a matter of fact, I did poison the drink.

Alex What?

Frances I poisoned her G & T.

Edward Why?

Frances Like you said. I hated her. I wanted her dead, so I poisoned her drink. I was sleeping with a chemist at the time. He told me what to do.

Edward So, wait a minute, you...admit you murdered her?

Frances Not at all.

Alex But you just said you poisoned her!

Frances No, I poisoned her drink. Not her.

Edward How absolute the knave is.

Frances You see, there's a subtle difference.

Alex Too subtle for me.

Frances She never drank it.

Edward How can you be sure?

Frances Because the drink that Ruby had just before she disappeared upstairs wasn't hers. It was Hedley's.

Edward Hedley's?

Frances Yes. She stole it from him.

Hedley Oh, yes. I remember that.

Edward How the hell would you remember a thing like that?

Hedley Because I was having a blazing row with Ruby when Frances handed her the drink. She tipped it straight over my head, and then pinched my glass and stormed off upstairs.

Ruby That's true, unfortunately.

Frances Hours of planning and twenty quid's worth of poison down the drain. And all that happened was that Hedley's wig shrivelled up.

Hedley It is not a wig.

Frances No, of course not, Hedley. It's an over-friendly hamster.

Ruby Can you believe my luck? I throw away a poisoned drink and pick up another one.

Frances So, there you have it. There's my confession.

Edward But at the very least, you're guilty of attempted murder!

Frances Am I? I thought we were just discussing this hypothetically, for the purposes of the play.

Edward Well, yes, we were, but...

Frances Well, there you are then. I've done my bit. I'll expect a share of the writer's royalties.

Ruby I can't believe how cool she is.

Edward All right. So what are we saying now, hypothetically? That there were two lethal cocktails?

Glenda And the second one was meant for poor old Hedley.

Hedley Bastards.

Alex The first was meant for Ruby and ended up on Hedley. The second was meant for Hedley and ended up in Ruby.

Edward But who hated Hedley enough to kill him?

Alex Ruby did.

Frances She's hardly likely to poison Hedley's drink and then drink it herself.

Glenda Unless it was suicide.

Edward No, it wasn't suicide.

Glenda How can you be sure?

Edward She told me.

Glenda That's fair enough.

Alex So, we're back to square one. Everybody hates Hedley.

Hedley Cheers.

Edward Not quite back to square one. You see, by calculating the time of death, the writer has deduced that his wife could only have been murdered by one of three people. Howard, who unfortunately isn't here to defend himself. Frances, who's already admitted to trying but failing - hypothetically, of course. And you, Hedley.

Hedley Frankly Edward, I think this whole bloody business is in very bad taste.

Ruby I think he's cracking!

Frances How can you talk about bad taste, wearing a tie like that?

Edward What do you mean, Hedley?

Hedley Your wife's barely been dead a year, and here you are, writing ludicrous plot lines around her just to try and resurrect your flagging career.

Edward How dare you!

Frances Don't be ridiculous, Hedley. If he wanted to resurrect his career he would have written about somebody with a bit of charisma.

Ruby That's it!

Ruby grabs Hedley's wig, thrusts it into Frances' face, then drops it into her lap. She screams, stands up, tosses her drink onto the wig and starts stamping on it, as if it were a harmful rodent. Hedley, also panicking, tries to rescue it. Edward and Ruby take the chance for a quick aside.

Edward What the hell are you doing?

Ruby She asked for it. They both did!

Edward Stop interfering!

Hedley Leave my bloody hair alone!

Frances It attacked me! Did anybody see that? It went for my throat.

Alex All right, all right! Stand back. Leave it to me. *(He tentatively picks up the wig)* I think it's dead.

Glenda It was probably just a gust of wind.

Hedley I'll sue you for this.

Frances Try it. I'll have you arrested.

Hedley *Me* arrested? What the hell for?

Frances Dangerous Wigs Act. You need a bloody muzzle on your head.

Alex Put it back on, Hedley.

Frances Never mind putting it on. It wants putting down, if you ask me.

Hedley Bloody maniac.

Hedley hastily stuffs it back on. It's wet, dishevelled and the wrong way round.

Frances Look at him. Drunk in charge of a hairpiece.

Edward Calm down everybody. My fault. I left the window open. *(He shuts it)* There you go. Should be all right now. Let's get on with the play.

Hedley Stuff the bloody play. The whole thing's in bad taste, and I'm having nothing more to do with it.

Frances You can count me out too.

Alex Now look! I think it took a lot of courage for Edward to write this play. It's been a traumatic experience for him. But if he can go through with it, so can we.

Besides, I'd rather like to see how it ends, wouldn't you?

Frances I don't need the work.

Alex Of course not, Frances. But artistically, this could be your greatest triumph yet.

Ruby That wouldn't be difficult.

Edward There is another consideration, of course. Anybody who walks out now could be viewed with a degree of suspicion.

Glenda has got up and is heading for the door. She stops and turns as she feels the weight of the others' stares on her back.

Glenda (*haughtily*) Toilet.

She struts out indignantly.

Edward (*pointing to the other door*) It's that way, Glenda.

Alex Well, Frances?

Frances All right, let's press on.

Alex Hedley?

Hedley What the hell. Roll the dice.

Alex Brilliant. Can I get anyone another drink?

Hedley If you're in the chair, I'll just have a small half.

Alex Half a bottle for Hedley? Anyone else?

Frances Another large wine for me. The first glass seems to have gone straight to his head.

Glenda enters in a daze.

Alex Glenda?

Glenda Forget it.

Alex Another drink?

Glenda (*handing over her empty pint glass*) Oh! Just another small sherry, please.

Alex Right.

Glenda (*to Alex*) Shall I give you a hand?

Frances No, I'll go. You go and make room for it. The toilet's through that door, darling.

Glenda Right.

They all hand glasses to Alex and Frances, who exit.

A Flying Ducks Publication

Hedley Well, I suppose under the circumstances, I ought to make a confession.
Edward Confession?
Hedley I didn't really want any of this to come out, but, well, I don't see any choice now.
Ruby This could be it!
Edward Go on, Hedley.
Hedley The fact is, I do wear a wig.

Edward offers a dumbfounded stare.

Hedley I can see that's shocked you.
Edward I'm speechless.
Hedley Good. Because it's not something I particularly like talking about. And now that it's all out in the open, I'd appreciate it if we could let the subject drop.
Edward Fine.
Hedley Can I rely on you to keep it to ourselves?
Edward Of course, Hedley. It'll just be our little secret.
Ruby Us and the rest of the sighted population. Uh!
Edward What?
Ruby Oh, no. Not this soon. Please.
Edward Ruby? What's wrong?
Ruby Got to go.
Edward Ruby! Ruby!!

She disappears offstage. Edward becomes aware that he is being stared at by Hedley.

Edward Sorry. I was...just acting out a scene...from the play. An idea for an ending.

Alex and Frances enter with drinks for all, and start handing them out.

Alex Drinks everybody.
Frances Having a bad hair day, Hedley?
Edward Don't start that again, please.
Frances There's yours, Hedley. That's Glenda's there.

During the next speech, Glenda wanders in sheepishly, and picks up Hedley's drink by mistake.

Alex Let me just remind everyone why we're here. And it's not to tear each other apart. Edward's worked very hard on this. And if it's a winner, we could all stand to make a lot of money. Let's face it. We're not all exactly inundated with work at the moment are we?

Frances Speak for yourself, darling.

Alex Do you want the job, or not?

Frances I suppose I could squeeze it in, just to help out.

Alex Right. Then, I'd like to propose a toast. To Edward's new play. May it run and run.

All Edward's new play.

They all swig. Glenda and Hedley both grimace.

Hedley Uggh! Sherry!

Glenda Whisky!

They swap drinks.

Frances There's just one problem. What are we going to do about the ending?

Alex Ah, yes, the ending. Well, I've got an idea for that.

Frances Oh, let us in on the secret.

Alex The play's the thing, wherein I'll catch the conscience of the king. That was Hamlet's plan, wasn't it? To put on a play which mirrors the murder, and then watch for signs of guilt on the face of the king.

Frances So?

Alex So, Edward thought he'd use the same ploy to flush out his wife's murderer.

Edward Did I?

Alex Except, of course, he hasn't got the help of a real ghost.

Edward No. Not at the moment.

Alex The play's the thing, wherein I'll catch the conscience of...(*looking at Hedley*) the king. Or could it be, (*moving to Frances*)...the queen?

Frances I've already laid my cards on the table.

Alex Wrong type of queen, darling.

Edward What are you trying to say, Alex?

Alex The classic whodunit. Who's the least obvious suspect?

Glenda I suppose I am. As I wasn't even there.

Alex Neither was I, apparently. Migraine. Left early. Pretty pathetic, though, isn't it? How easy it would have been for me to slip back unnoticed and do the dirty deed.

Edward You?

Alex The hero's devoted gay friend, secretly incensed by his blind love for his wife. He saw what she was doing to him. And he'd do anything to save him.

Edward Anything?

Alex (*an earnest, emotional exchange*) She was no good for you, Edward.

Edward You've made that perfectly clear.

Alex She was destroying your talent.

Edward So you destroyed her?

Alex I loved you more than she ever could! (*Leaving Edward perplexed, he twists back to a whimsical mood*) Well, what do you think?

Frances Plausible, I suppose.

Glenda I think it's terrific.

Alex But have I convinced the writer?

Edward Are you playing games with me?

Alex Just trying to help you think of an ending, Edward. You said you wanted our help.

Hedley Hang on a minute. Is he saying he's gay?

Frances Good Lord, no, Hedley. Alex is only pretending to be gay. Just like you're only pretending to be bald.

Hedley Christ. I've shared dressing rooms with him.

Alex (*putting his arm around Hedley*) He hath borne me on his back a thousand times.

Hedley (*pushing him off*) No he bloody hasn't!

Alex All right, all right. Keep your hair on.

Glenda I think I need to use the bathroom again.

Edward Come on.

While Hedley blusters at Alex, Edward leads Glenda to the bathroom door. He opens it and lets out a stifled scream, which scares everyone into reacting. They all stare at Edward for an explanation.

Edward (*pointing pathetically*) Erm...big spider. In the bath. Can you cope?

Glenda I'll just be sick on him.

As Glenda exits into the bathroom, Ruby enters from it.

Ruby Big spider indeed!

Edward Welcome back.

Ruby Last time, I'm afraid.

Alex So, what do you think, maestro?

Edward What?

Alex My ending.

Edward The gay lover.

Alex The gay spurned lover. Let's leave the hero's macho reputation intact.

Ruby I hate to say it, but this puts Alex right back in the frame.

Edward Terrific. We start with a shortlist of three suspects, and narrow it down to four.

Alex Just trying to help.

Edward All right, then. Help me some more. If he did do it, how do we find out?

Alex Oh, that's easy. He just comes right out with it.

Edward And why would he do that?

Alex Because he knows you'll never tell anyone.

Edward Why not?

Alex Because deep down this isn't a comedy. It's a tragedy. Like Hamlet. And we all know what happens at the end of tragedies.

Hedley They all drop dead.

Alex Quite.

Frances Poisoned drinks.

Alex Exactly.

Hedley Not bad.

They all suddenly reflect in horror on the fact that they've been sipping drinks offered by Alex. Frances suddenly groans and slumps.

Frances The drink! The drink! I am...poisoned.

She collapses dramatically. The others crowd around her, concerned - all except Hedley, who is unconvinced.

Hedley You always were crap at that scene, Frances. Put some bloody soul into it, woman. (*He stands and demonstrates with some very flamboyant ham stage acting*) "O, I die, Horatio: the potent poison quite o'erflows my spirit. Wretched queen, adieu! The rest is...silent!"

Hedley slumps back into his chair. The others ignore him, but are still genuinely concerned by the state of Frances.

Edward Frances. Frances!

Alex Something's wrong.

Alex jumps up and heads for the door.

Edward Where the hell do you think you're going?
Alex To call an ambulance.
Edward You're not going anywhere. Glenda!
Alex What have I done?
Edward Oh, not much! You've practically admitted to poisoning her!
Alex Oh, come on! That was just a joke. An idea! To help the play!

Glenda totters in.

Glenda I don't feel very well.
Edward Quickly! Phone for an ambulance.
Glenda No, I'll be all right.
Edward Not for you! Frances has been poisoned!
Glenda Shit!

Glenda rushes back into the bathroom.

Edward Glenda!

She rushes back out.

Glenda Where's the phone?
Alex Hall, downstairs.
Glenda Right.

She dashes out of the other door, but is instantly called back by Edward.

Edward Glenda!
Glenda What?
Edward Use mine.
Glenda Where?
Edward Under the bed.

*Glenda delves under the bed and frantically starts tossing out a few unsavoury objects -
old sandwich, Chinese food containers, etc. She finally unearths a phone hidden*

inside an old pair of underpants. She pulls the receiver through the hole in the underpants and dials.

Glenda Emergency. Underpants, please. No, ambulance, you stupid man!
Edward And Police!
Glenda And Police.

Frances suddenly jumps up.

Frances Had you going there for a minute, didn't I?
Edward Bloody hell, Frances! You sod!
Frances The power of real acting, darling.
Glenda (*slamming down the phone*) Sorry. False alarm. Forget it.
Edward That was evil.
Glenda Is Hedley all right?
Alex He's just passed out.
Ruby Passed on, you mean. No pulse.
Edward What? (*He rushes over to Hedley*) He's dead!
Alex He can't be!
Frances Died of over-acting probably.
Ruby His drink's been poisoned.
Edward Are you sure?
Frances It was just a joke, darling.
Ruby Positive. Same stuff as did for me. Still, shame to waste it. (*She takes a big swig*)
Edward Glenda, call an ambulance!
Glenda I don't feel well.
Alex What good's an ambulance? He's dead!
Edward Call the police then!
Glenda I feel sick.
Edward Oh, come here, I'll do it!
Ruby No!
Edward I've got to call the police!
Alex Get on with it, then!
Ruby But we're so close! Don't you see? This rules out Howard, because he's not here. And it rules out Hedley. Because he's dead! It could only be Frances or Alex. Just give me another few minutes to work it out. Please?
Edward Police!

Ruby, desperate to stop the call, yanks out the cable from the wall. She stands behind Edward's ear, pinching her nose, imitating the sound of the telephone operator.

Ruby Police, can I help you?
Edward Oh, yes, we need the police, now. There's been a murder.
Alex Murder?
Ruby Oh, I see, sir. And what kind of murder might that be?
Edward What do you mean, what kind of murder? A very naughty one. Just get over here, now! Flat 2B, Elsinore Gardens.
Ruby What's the rush?
Edward What's the bloody rush? There's a dead man in my lounge!
Ruby Well he's not going anywhere is he.
Edward I'm sharing a room with a bloody murderer! How would you like it?
Ruby All right, all right. We'll get someone over here just as soon as we can.
Edward Over here?
Ruby Over there, to where you are. Got to go. Busy night.

She imitates the "click, brrrr..." of the receiver going down.

Edward Thanks a bunch. Whatever happened to the village bobby?
Glenda My stomach!
Edward What the hell do you expect, drinking a pint of sherry?
Alex What did you mean, murder?
Edward Don't play the innocent with me, pal. His drink was poisoned.
Alex What?
Edward The same poison that killed Ruby.

Glenda collapses in agony, clutching her stomach.

Glenda Help me!
Alex Glenda, darling, no-one's going to feel sympathy for you if you drink...drink!
   She had a sip of Hedley's drink!
Edward Shit!
Alex I'm calling an ambulance.
Edward Frances! Help me get her on the bed!

While Frances and Edward struggle to get Glenda onto the bed, Alex picks up the phone, realises there's no dialling tone, then sees the wire is pulled out of the socket.

Alex So, you phoned the police, did you?
Edward They're on their way.
Alex Are they now! (*He shows Edward the bare wire*) What the hell's going on?
Edward I'll kill her!
Ruby I'm already dead, sweetie.
Edward I'll use your phone.
Alex You're not going anywhere!
Edward Oh, terrific, now I'm a suspect!
Alex I'll go.
Edward You're not going anywhere.
Ruby Sort it out! She's dying.
Frances Stop arguing - I'll go.

Frances gets as far as opening the door, but is called back by Alex. She leaves the door wide open.

Alex Wait a minute. She's not going anywhere.
Glenda For God's sake, one of you get the bloody ambulance!
Edward What the problem now?
Alex She poisoned the drink.
Frances That's nonsense.
Alex It's true.
Edward How do you know.
Alex Because I know I didn't.
Frances He's lying.
Alex Come on, Edward. One of us has to go. Use your instinct.

A tense moment of deliberation. Edward looks to Ruby.

Ruby Sorry, sweetie. I can't help you.
Edward Alex.....go and phone.
Frances (*reaching for the pistol she has spotted in Edward's room*) Hold it! You're not going anywhere!
Ruby Bingo! We've got her! Well done, sweetie!
Edward Frances, that's not even a real...
Alex All right, Edward, leave this to me.
Edward Ambulance, Alex!
Ruby Wait! Please Edward. Just ask her why. I need to know why!
Edward Why, Frances?

Frances O cursed spite, that ever I was born to set it right!

Edward What?

Frances He destroyed the life of someone very dear to me. A young actress, the brightest talent at college. Could have gone right to the top. But she was naive. Thought she could learn something from the experienced actor who kindly offered her private lessons at home. Oh, she learned something all right. She learned what it's like to be seduced by a drunken old hack when you're just eighteen years old.

Edward Look, I'm sure this is a great story, Frances. But Glenda needs an ambulance.

Frances Shut up! I haven't finished yet. Where was I?

Alex Young actress. Eighteen years old.

Frances Oh, yes. And pregnant. Too embarrassed to even tell her mother, she ran away from her comfortable, loving, middle-class home. When she should have been playing Ophelia, she was washing nappies, working in a burger bar to pay the rent. He stole the best years of her life. And now, I bet he couldn't even remember the name of that promising young actress.

Alex My God. Lucy. Your daughter.

Frances No, me you bitch! This was thirty years ago.

Edward Look, I can understand you hating Hedley. Even Ruby. But Glenda's never hurt you. Give her a chance to live.

Frances Why? So she can steal my part at the next audition?

Ruby God she's bitter! I thought I knew how to bear a grudge!

Alex So what are you going to do with us?

Frances Well, like the man said, it's turned out to be a bit of a tragedy.

Alex Come on, Frances, you wouldn't shoot me.

She shoots him. He gasps, and staggers to the floor clutching his stomach. Then, he jumps up.

Alex You bloody well would as well, wouldn't you!

Frances screams, and runs for the open door. Ruby shuts it in time for her to crash into it. She smashes her nose and collapses to the floor.

Ruby Allow me to show you the door.

Edward The ambulance!

Alex I'll go.

Alex exits.

A Flying Ducks Publication

Edward Come on, Glenda! She's hardly got any pulse.
Ruby (*checking her pulse*) I think you're going to lose her, sweetie.
Edward Oh, no!
Ruby Sorry, just a feeling. You're quite fond of her, aren't you?
Edward This is no time to get jealous, Ruby.
Ruby I'm not. I was being sincere. You just didn't recognise it.
Edward It just gets...lonely out here sometimes.
Ruby I know. I know.
Edward She's stopped breathing. Shit! What do I do?
Ruby Kiss of life. Bang her chest.

Edward frantically tries to revive Glenda.

Edward Come on, Glenda. Fight! Please! Don't leave me, Glenda. Breathe.
Come on, Glenda. Breathe. Hang on!

*A dramatic drone of music builds, and a spotlight closes on Ruby, her eyes staring
eerily forward as she remembers the fateful night she was murdered. Edward, now a
shadowy silhouette in the background, desperately tries to revive the figure on the bed,
but his words have changed.*

Edward Come on, Ruby. Fight! Please! Don't leave me, Ruby. Breathe. Come
on, Ruby. Hang on!
Ruby She's dead. Can't you see? It's no use! She's dead!

*Ruby looks to the skies and lets out an angry, blood-curdling cry. There's a mighty
thunderclap, and the windows rattle open. Ominous music and a terrible storm
underpin the action. The lighting is surreal, punctuated by lightning flashes. Frances,
who was trying to crawl unnoticed out of the door, can suddenly see and hear Ruby.
She freezes in terror, as Ruby points to her and assumes a terrifying voice.*

Ruby Remember me!!
Frances No!
Ruby How now, Frances?
Frances Ruby?
Ruby You tremble and look pale: Is this not something more than fantasy?
Edward Ruby! What are you doing?
Ruby Clause Thirteen. The bee sting.

A Flying Ducks Publication

Edward Don't do it!

Frances I..I didn't mean to kill you, Ruby, it was an accident. We were always such
good friends...

Ruby O most pernicious woman! O villain, villain, smiling, damned villain!

Frances Arrrrrgh!

Frances, stalked by Ruby, has backed away in terror to the open window, and with a
scream she topples backwards and falls out. Ruby stands on the window frame looking
down. The surreal lighting effects suggest she is standing on the gateway to Hell.

Ruby My hour is almost come when I to sulphurous and tormenting flames must
render up myself.

Edward No!

Ruby It is time. Sint mihi dei Acherontis propitii.

Edward I'm coming with you.

Ruby No! Finish the play!

Edward There's nothing for me here!

Ruby Glenda needs you!

Edward Ruby!

Ruby Adieu, adieu, adieu! Remember me!

Edward (*with a blood-curdling scream*) Ruby!!!

Ruby jumps down from the window, disappearing, and at exactly the same time Glenda
screams and sits bolt upright on the bed, as if she's emerged from a nightmare. The
thunderclaps, storm and dramatic music suddenly stop and the lighting returns to
normal. A distant police siren can be heard from the street below, a blue flashing light
plays on the net curtains.

Edward Glenda?

Glenda Oh, Edward!

She runs to him and starts hugging and kissing him emotionally, much to Edward's
bewilderment.

Edward It's all right. Calm down.

Glenda I thought I'd gone.

Edward I know. It's okay. You're safe now.

Alex bursts in.

Alex Edward, the....oh, sorry.

Glenda breaks away.

Edward It's all right. She er...she seems better.
Alex Yes. Where's Frances?
Edward (*pointing down*) Erm....down there, somewhere.
Alex Oh. The police are here.
Edward Yes, I know. What the hell am I going to tell them?

Glenda turns.

Glenda Don't worry, sweetie. I'll explain everything.

Glenda exits, leaving Alex and Edward exchanging dumbfounded stares. Suddenly, their attention is taken by the typewriter, which bursts into life, typing up a final page.

Lights fade to black. Curtain.

A Flying Ducks Publication